SMILE

Milena Gilbreath

Copyright © 2019 by Milena Gilbreath.

ISBN   Softcover   978-1-949723-70-0

All rights reserved. No part of this book may be reproduced or transmitted in any form or by any means, electronic or mechanical, including photocopying, recording, or by any information storage and retrieval system without express written permission from the author, except in the case of brief quotations embodied in critical reviews and certain other non-commercial uses permitted by copyright law.

Printed in the United States of America.

To order additional copies of this book, contact:
Bookwhip
1-855-339-3589
https://www.bookwhip.com

To my son Garrett, husband Mel and family,
The girls in my chat group, **SMILE**,
and to Brenda Colalillo a friend
who always puts a smile on my face

WHAT IS A **SMILE** ?

A facial expression showing

pleasure, amusement, affection, etc, etc.

Now close your eyes and think of all the things that make you

SMILE

Tons of things right ?

Some Major Events such as your FIRST KISS,

Your first pair of HIGH HEELS.

Or simpler stuff like

The mouthwatering smell of delivery pizza,

Watching a sunset

Life's full of moments that make you

Breakout into a GOOFY grin just

Thinking about them.

So when you need a boost in your day,
Sit back relax, turn to any page in the book and

SMILE

SMILE WHEN

Finding a pair of jeans that make you look HOT.

Getting asked out by the guy you've been LUSTING after the moment you laid eyes on him.

SMILE
WHEN

Checking out the HOTTIES at the beach with your dark sunglasses on so they don't know you're watching..

Scoring tickets to your favorite band's concert and going ABSOLUTELY NUTS when they play all their best.

SMILE WHEN

Planning your next GREAT ADVENTURE to Europe with close friends.

Getting a GIFT CARD to your favorite store, and going on a wild guilt-free shopping spree.

SMILE WHEN

Trying something TOTALLY different, like chopping off your long locks for that short chic do

GO!

Eating anything with PEANUT BUTTER and CHOCOLATE in it, sweet!

SMILE WHEN

Raiding your SUPER GLAM friend's closet to find that perfect outfit you need.

Shaking what YOUR MAMA GAVE YOU as the D.J. plays all your favorites.

SMILE WHEN

Long BEACH STROLL in the sand
with your sweetie.

Showing off your legs in NEW HIGH HEELS
after you've been working out everyday.

SMILE WHEN

A JEWELRY find that looks like a million bucks on you, but cost only five dollars.

Laughing so hard with FRIENDS that you get a great abs workout.

SMILE
WHEN

A hot pair of sunglasses that make you feel
LIKE A STAR ever time you slip them on.

Blasting your BEST CD while getting ready to go out
on a Saturday night.

SMILE WHEN

Trying out new foods , who knew that
SUSHI could actually be so delish?

The look on your brothers face when you beat
him at tennis AGAIN !

SMILE WHEN

Licking fluffy PINK FROSTING off your lips as you finish that huge cupcake.

Lounging on the beach with girlfriends trading weekly gossip and watching all the CUTE GUYS go by.

SMILE
WHEN

Smelling the FAMILIAR SCENT of your home when you return from a long trip abroad .

Seeing your guy's JAW DROP when opening the door in HOT new dress.

SMILE WHEN

Having a good ol' cry while watching
a real TEARJERKER
movie with the girls at home.

Getting SPA TREATMENTS facials, manis,
and pedis that make you feel totally relaxed
and pampered, so nice.

SMILE WHEN

Getting into a GREAT BOOK, you can't even think of putting down till every single page has been read.

Wearing a FLIRTY DRESS to a casual event just to spice things up a little.

SMILE
WHEN

Chilling in a warm SCENTED BUBBLE BATH after a long stress filled day.

Snuggling close with your sweetie as you watch major LIGHTING BOLTS tearing across the sky.

SMILE WHEN

Having COMFORT FOODS like grilled cheese, chicken soup or
MAC and Cheese made for you when feeling sick.

That FIRST WARM DAY when you can't wait to get on your tee with shorts and sandals, FINALLY.

SMILE WHEN

Enjoying FAMILY RITUALS like Chinese takeout on Fridays and movie nights on Saturdays.

Programming that HOT NEW GUY'S number into your cell phone, FINALLY.

SMILE WHEN

Running into a old friend and realizing that TRUE FRIENDSHIP never ends.

Fresh WARM TOWELS right out of the dryer.

SMILE WHEN

Waking up on SUNDAY MORNING and having a huge breakfast with the whole family.

Jumping into a pool on a HOT DAY with all your clothes on!

SMILE
WHEN

Hearing your guy finally mumble the words
I LOVE YOU for the first time, wow.

Whipping up a VANILLA or CHOCOLATE
MILKSHAKE so thick you just have to use a spoon!

SMILE WHEN

Snuggling under lots of thick warm blankets on a COLD winter night.

Hitting a yard sale and finding a fabulous FAUX FUR JACKET, sweet.

SMILE WHEN

Enjoying the first big SNOW DAY outside then coming in for hot chocolate with marshmallows nice.

Your hair FINALLY falls just the way you want it to.

SMILE WHEN

Meeting SOMEONE NEW and knowing that she's going to be a great friend.

Getting a SUNNY DAY when the weatherman said it would rain.

SMILE
WHEN

A friend goes out of her way to
do SOMETHING SPECIAL for you.

The instant your FAVORITE SONG
plays you jump up and start dancing.

SMILE WHEN

A CUTE GUY flashes you a shy
smile as he passes by you.

Riding the MONSTER ROLLER COASTER ride
and screaming your head off the entire way down.

SMILE WHEN

Having CHOCOLATE as a friend, easy to get to
never talks back to you and always puts
a smile on your face.

Celebrating your birthday with TONS of
presents, cake, family and friends.

SMILE
WHEN

Finding TWENTY BUCKS in the pocket of jeans you haven't worn in ages.

Warm FUDGY BROWNIES with a cold glass of milk waiting on the counter for you when you get in.

SMILE WHEN

Hitting a cafe with GIRLFRIENDS and catching up with everyone over coffee and desserts.

When your sweetie brings you PINK ROSES just because.

SMILE WHEN

Taking long walks to calm you
down and clear your head.

Getting a THREE DAY weekend to
yourself and doing whatever, yes.

SMILE
WHEN

Finding a PARKING SPOT by the mall entrance on the busiest day of the year.

Sitting down in your FAVORITE chair, feet up sipping a cup of tea and reading the book.

So what makes you SMILE?

"Have always loved to read and write,
A passion encouraged early by my mother,
to follow my dreams. Enjoy and smile."

Find it and Do it Go!

Milena Gilbreath

Born in Toronto, Ontario, Canada, reside here with son and husband. Always loved reading and writing from a young age. Started with writing poetry first and now the next phase the writing of this book, so enjoy and

SMILE

www.ingramcontent.com/pod-product-compliance
Lightning Source LLC
Chambersburg PA
CBHW030133100526
44591CB00009B/632